ANCIENT ROME

Ancient Rome

CHARLES ALEXANDER ROBINSON, JR.
REVISED BY LORNA GREENBERG

A First Book | Revised Edition
FRANKLIN WATTS | 1984
New York | London | Toronto | Sydney

FRONTIS:
THE ROMAN FORUM

Maps by Vantage Art, Inc.

Cover photograph courtesy of
Photo Researchers, Inc. (George Holton)

Photographs courtesy of
Italian Government Travel Office: frontispiece, pp. 8, 42, 52;
Italian Cultural Institute: pp. 4, 22, 28, 32, 34, 48;
Alissa Greenberg: p. 12; Metropolitan Museum of Art, Rogers Fund:
pp. 16 (1913), 38 (1903); Ron Greenberg: p. 40

Library of Congress Cataloging in Publication Data

Robinson, Charles Alexander, 1900-1965.
Ancient Rome.

(A First book)
Includes index.
Bibliography: p.
Summary: An account of life in ancient Rome, from its founding
through the rise of Christianity and the fall of the Roman Empire,
including its history, art, and important people.
1. Rome—History—Juvenile literature. [1. Rome—
Civilization] I. Greenberg, Lorna. II. Title.
DG210.R62 1984   937   83-21573
ISBN 0-531-04728-8

CONTENTS

FOR MY GRANDCHILDREN

THE FOUNDING OF ROME

For many centuries Italy has been a center of civilization. Rome, the chief city of Italy, created the largest empire the ancient world ever saw. Nearly all the civilized world was a part of the Roman Empire. That meant that everyone from Britain to Persia (now Iran) was part of one community. They were all protected by the same armies and tried by the same laws, and all paid taxes into the same treasury.

The Roman civilization lasted for about a thousand years. When the Empire finally fell, great modern nations such as England, France, and Italy itself grew from its fragments and kept alive many of its achievements.

The land of Italy, where the Roman civilization grew, begins just south of the Swiss Alps and soon becomes a peninsula running to the southeast between the Adriatic and the Mediterranean seas. The peninsula is about 750 miles (1,206 km) long, and rarely more than 125 miles (201 km) wide. The Apennine Mountains run down the length of the peninsula like a spine and at places rise to a height of over 9,500 feet (2,896 m).

The most famous river is the Tiber, where Rome is located. The city was not built where the Tiber empties into the Mediterranean, for that would be open to attacks by pirates. It was built 15 miles (24 km) up the river. Ancient boats could navigate that far, and at that point there was an island which made it easier to cross the river.

[1]

Rome's location in central Italy, near the sea and controlling the ford of the Tiber, meant that trade rapidly became important. There was some level ground beside the river, where people could meet and exchange goods. In time the Romans turned this into their marketplace, or Forum, with law courts, temples to the gods, and shops. Surrounding the Forum were the Seven Hills of Rome. The most important of these were the Capitoline, where the city's original fort was located, and the Palatine, where powerful emperors later built their palaces.

The beginnings of Rome stretch far back through history to very early times—long before the days of any clear records. As Rome grew to become a center of importance, a legendary history collected around it, to explain how and why Rome began, and to show that, from the first, it was fated to become a great civilization. This history, with traces of actual events mixed with legends from the Greeks, Etruscans, and the Latin tribes of the region, came to be the traditional version of the founding of Rome.

The beginning of the story is rooted in Greek legends that describe how the Greeks besieged the city of Troy for ten long years. At last, about 1184 B.C., the city fell. One of the few Trojan survivors was the hero Aeneas, son of the goddess Aphrodite. He fled burning Troy bearing his aged father on his shoulders and leading his young son, Ascanius.

The Roman poet Virgil continues the tale. He tells how Aeneas wandered for seven years until he at last reached the region called Latium, on the west coast of the Italian peninsula, where lived a tribe of people called Latins. Aeneas married the king of the tribe's daughter, and succeeded the king as ruler of the Latins. Later his son founded a town called Alba Longa, in the Alban Hills, 19 miles (30.5 km) from the future city of Rome.

Alba Longa became the capital of Latium and was ruled for centuries by the descendents of Aeneas. In the eighth century B.C. the throne was seized by the rightful king's younger brother, Amulius. Soon after, the true king's daughter gave birth to twin boys and said they had been fathered by the god Mars. Amulius feared they might someday claim the throne and ordered them drowned in the River Tiber. But the infants—Romulus and Remus—were washed ashore. For a time they were suckled by a she-wolf and fed by a woodpecker. At last, the shepherd Faustulus found them and raised them in his home.

Years later the boys proved the evil king Amulius's fears true. They returned to Alba Longa, killed him, and placed their grandfather on the throne. Then they set out—with a band of landless men as followers—to found their own city at the edge of the Tiber, where the she-wolf had rescued them. But the brothers quarreled over the site of their city, and Remus was killed. So Romulus alone began his city, according to legend, in 753 B.C.

His settlement grew quickly, for everyone was welcome: young men with no property or prospects, debtors, runaway slaves, and others. But it was a colony of men only. Perhaps to provide wives for his followers, Romulus invited the neighboring tribes, including the Sabines, to a festival. In the midst of the ceremonies, Romulus and his men seized the Sabine women and carried them off. The angry Sabine men tried to rescue the women but had little success. At last a truce was made between the Sabines and the Romans. They agreed to form one people, ruled jointly by Romulus and the Sabine chief. When the Sabine died, Romulus continued to rule—for thirty-seven years in all—until he mysteriously disappeared in the midst of a frightful storm.

From this multicolored fabric of legend, it is fascinating to seek the threads of history. We know that by about 1000 B.C. a number of Indo-European tribes had moved down into the Italian peninsula—conquering, mixing with, and sometimes displacing the peoples who had centuries earlier—during the ice age—entered the region as roving hunter-gatherers and then gradually settled and formed small farming communities. One of the last tribes to enter Italy were the Latins, who settled in the Alban Hills, in the plain of Latium, south of the Tiber. These were the people who were to become the Romans.

By the eighth century B.C. there were clusters of mud-hut villages scattered over the seven hills around the Tiber. As the settlements spread down the hills, the tribespeople met on the marshy plains between them. This open area, outside the limits of the separate villages on the hills, became a common ground—a Forum (from the Latin, meaning "place outside the door")—where the early settlers could meet and trade. In time it would become the heart of the vast Roman Empire.

**Romulus and Remus—
the legendary twins
rescued by a she-wolf
—became the symbol
of ancient Rome.**

ROME IN THE AGE OF KINGS

From the works of Roman historians we can re-create the traditional (still partly legendary) history of the early days of Rome. According to early writers, Rome was ruled by a series of seven kings from 753 B.C., when Romulus founded Rome, to about 509 B.C., when the era of the rule by kings ended.

Under the kings, the political institutions that were to shape the Roman state began to appear. The king was the head of the state. He was elected from within the royal family and held the authority to rule, called the *imperium*. The symbol of this power was the *fasces*, a small bundle of wooden rods surrounding an axe. The king had many officials to carry out the work of governing the state. The second branch of the state government was the Senate (from the Latin *senatus*, "old men"), a council of elders chosen by the king to be advisors. An assembly of the people, the Comitia Curiata, was the third part. This popular assembly is the oldest known Roman assembly and was made up of all citizens capable of bearing arms. Two other assemblies were introduced later, the Comitia Centuriata and the Comitia Tributa. Each was based on a different system of organizing the citizens.

Under the rule of the first four kings, Rome grew to be the chief city in Latium. Then with the next ruler, two strong foreign influences entered the Roman world. This king, Tarquinius Priscus, was not a Latin or a Sabine as the earlier kings had been. He was half Greek and half Etruscan (although he is called an Etruscan king), and thus represented two strong elements that would influence Rome in the coming centuries—the Etruscans and the Greeks. Beginning about 750 B.C., the overpopulated city-states of Greece had sent colonists westward to found new cities. So many of these colonists settled in southern Italy that the region came to be called Magna Graecia, "Great Greece." While there were no Greek colonies closer to Rome than the Bay of Naples, active trade links brought the Romans under the influence of Greek culture and ideas.

The other foreign (non-Italian) influence was the Etruscans, a fascinating, strong people of mysterious origins who began to appear on the west coast of Italy around 800 B.C. Today we are still not sure where they came from. Herodotus, the fifth century B.C. Greek historian, declared they came from Lydia, in Asia Minor. Other writers have said they were a people who had lived in Italy from earliest times. We do know they were a highly civilized people, much ahead of the Italian tribes of the region. They were skilled farmers, merchants, sailors, builders, soldiers, and colonizers. They were fond of music and dancing, and enjoyed luxury.

The Etruscans settled in central Italy in a section later known as Etruria. Today this area is called Tuscany, and its chief city is Florence. The Etruscans, like the Romans, learned a good deal from the Greeks, with whom they traded actively. They adopted some Greek gods, along with the gods' legends, and the Greek alphabet, which they used to write their own language. The vivid wall paintings uncovered in Etruscan tombs have inscriptions written with Greek characters. We can now read some of the words, but do not yet understand the structure of the language. The Romans then borrowed their alphabet from the Etruscans, and adapted it to Latin.

Beginning with Tarquinius Priscus, the last three kings of Rome were Etruscan. Tarquinius Priscus became Rome's ruler at the end of the seventh century B.C. and began to introduce Etrus-

[7]

Pompeii, in the southern part of the Italian peninsula,
was an ancient settlement that fell under Greek influence.
Later, when the Romans moved south, they gained
control of Pompeii. A large and prosperous city grew up
here—under the shadow of Mt. Vesuvius.

can ideas. Temples were built to Etruscan gods. Later these gods, with some slight name changes (Tinia became the Roman Jupiter, Uni became Juno, Menerva became Minerva), were adopted into Roman beliefs. Using Etruscan engineering skills, the marshy Forum area was drained through a "Great Sewer," the Cloaca Maxima. The Circus Maximus was built, a racecourse where contests and games were held. Etruscan words, dances, music, clothing (the red military cloak worn by Roman generals, and the purple-edged toga of the nobles), and crafts all became permanent parts of the Roman world. Rome became a large, rich city of perhaps as many as 25,000 people spread through the seven hills. And, by taking over neighboring villages and tribes, Rome was beginning to grow into a nation.

THE REPUBLIC

Historical tradition holds that in 509 B.C., the Romans rebelled against the last Etruscan ruler, the cruel and ambitious Tarquin the Proud, and ended the rule of kings. Gradually, then, the Romans created their Republic, a state that was to endure for nearly 500 years, from 509 to 27 B.C.

To us, a republic is a state in which power to govern is held by the people, not by a king or ruler, and is then given to chosen representatives for a limited time. To the Romans, in the Republic, the rule of law replaced the rule of kings. The power to govern—the *imperium* that the kings had once held—was shared by two officials, consuls, who were elected for a term of one year. The consuls had equal power, and could "veto" (from the Latin, meaning "I forbid") each other's acts. In this way, no one person could become too powerful. At the end of their year in office, the consuls had to account to the Senate for what they had or had not accomplished. Under these chief executives were many officials—magistrates—who administered the government.

The Senate (as in the days of the kings) was the advisory body of the state. In time, its size was set at 300 members. The Senate was made up of members of the noble class who usually held their seats for life. This body nominated candidates, from among themselves, for the office of consul. An assembly of the people, the Comitia Centuriata, then elected the consuls.

An ambitious noble who hoped to become a consul first had to be elected to lower offices. After long service in different offices, he could stand for election as consul. He later could be named proconsul, or governor, of a district Rome ruled. Then for the rest of his life, he would be a member of the Senate.

The first centuries of the Republic were marked by a bitter class struggle within the state and almost constant fighting along its frontiers. From the times of the kings there had been two separate classes in Roman society: the patricians, or nobles, and the plebeians, or common people. Both groups were citizens, but the patricians (from the Latin *patres*, "fathers," or "heads of families") had greater privileges. The revolt against the kings had been led by the patricians, and in the early Republic, they tried to keep all privileges and powers within their own class. They filled the Senate and even controlled the votes in the Assembly. The plebeians, or plebs, had no voice in the state. They could not hold important offices or perform religious rituals, or marry patricians. The plebeians determined to gain some power and, beginning in 494 B.C., forced the patricians to meet first one demand and then another. One technique they used in their drive to gain economic and social equality was "to secede." A group of plebs moved out of Rome—where they claimed they had no place—and set up their own state. To persuade them to return and take up their duties as soldiers, farmers, and workers, the patricians first agreed to create a number of plebeian officials, called "tribunes," to defend the rights of the plebeians. After this victory, the plebs won the right to marry patricians, hold offices, have their own council—the Concilium Plebis—and make their own laws, and even serve as consul. The cruel laws of debt were softened, and the plebs gained a fairer share of state land. By 287 B.C. they had full and equal rights. However, none of this progress benefited the thousands of Roman slaves, who were not citizens and had no rights of any kind.

Through this period of internal struggle, the Romans were involved in constant battles to gain control of more and more territory. Rome sought to expand and extend its power, partly to

One of Rome's first colonies was Ostia, at the mouth of
the Tiber River. It grew to be an important port of Rome. Seventy
trading organizations from all over the ancient
world had offices there. Each office had a mosaic floor
with symbols designating where they came from or
what they traded. The elephant was the symbol of
traders from Sabrata, in North Africa.

defend itself against neighboring tribes, partly to gain land for its growing population, and partly because of aggressive leaders. So the Roman forces moved further and further out from Rome— taking over first the cities of Latium, then lands of other Italian tribes and of the Etruscans, until finally they controlled all of the region down to the Greek colonies in the south. After three huge battles, the Romans defeated the Greeks, too, about 275 B.C., and now ruled the whole Italian peninsula.

Once the Romans had conquered another people, they were usually tolerant of local customs, languages, and religions, and generous in their treatment of their former enemies. When peace was established, trade began to flourish. Latin and Italian tribes were allowed to manage their own affairs and only had to supply troops to Rome. Many settlements believed an alliance with Rome was valuable and provided them with protection.

THE PUNIC WARS

By 272 B.C., Rome was securely in control of the Italian Peninsula. But across the Mediterranean Sea from Italy, on the coast of North Africa, lay a rival power—the rich city-state of Carthage, ruler of the western Mediterranean. Carthage was a Phoenician—or as the Romans called it, a "Punic"—settlement. It had been founded about 800 B.C. by Phoenician colonists from Tyre. At first it was just a trading outpost, but in time it came to control its neighboring settlements and peoples, and all the commerce of the region. Carthage gradually built its own strong empire in North Africa and spread out to Spain and Sicily as well.

Trouble between Rome and Carthage first began in Sicily, where there were a good number of Greek colonies, some dating from the eighth century B.C., and some even-older Carthaginian settlements. Rome began to fear that Carthage might gain control of Sicily, and Carthaginian troops would then be too close to Roman southern Italy. By 264 B.C., Rome and Carthage had begun a long and bloody war which raged until 241 B.C., when Rome won a decisive sea battle. This was the first of the series of three Punic Wars between the rival states of Carthage and Rome.

Victorious Rome now took control of the island of Sicily—its first foreign province. Within a few years Rome also conquered the islands of Sardinia, Corsica, and then Corfu. On these islands the Romans were brought into close contact with the many Greek colonists who had settled there. This increased the Greek influence on Roman civilization, as the Romans were able to absorb and adapt many aspects of Greek culture. The Romans began to copy Greek forms in literature and art; they even merged Greek gods into their own. Roman gods took on the characters and the myths of similar Greek gods, and were then portrayed in sculpture in the same fashion as the Greek gods. The chief Roman God, Jupiter, took on qualities of Zeus, the Greek father-god; Juno, wife of Jupiter, took on qualities of Zeus's wife, Hera; Venus and the Greek Aphrodite, and Neptune and Poseidon were merged. Some Greek gods, such as Apollo, were adopted without a change in name. The Romans learned and benefited from the more advanced Greek culture during the period after the first Punic War, and it was a time of great growth for them.

But the peace with Carthage was only a truce. Carthage was bitter over its loss of Sicily, and needed new lands to supply sources of wealth (such as silver mines), and troops for its armies. An able Carthaginian general, Hamilcar Barca, pushed north into Spain in 236 B.C. and began to build a new Carthaginian empire from which to atttack Rome. Tradition says that before he sailed from Carthage, he took his then nine-year-old son, Hannibal, to a temple and had him swear to dedicate his life to the destruction of Rome. When Hannibal succeeded his father, as governor of what had become the mighty state of Carthaginian Spain, he set out to fulfill that vow.

Hannibal was one of the greatest generals of ancient times. With confidence in himself and his troops, he began his mission by seizing Saguntum, a city friendly to Rome. This action led to the outbreak of the terrible Second Punic War (218–201 B.C.), which was to decide who would control the western Mediterranean.

Hannibal had a simple, direct plan. He would lead his troops north from Spain, across the Alps, and then down into Italy— surprising the Romans by attacking from the north. He started in

218 B.C. with an army estimated at from 40,000 to 90,000 soldiers, and a herd of African forest elephants. He expected to be able to enlarge his army (and replace any losses) by winning over some of Rome's allies—tribes who were bound by treaty to supply troops to Rome. This would ensure him a supply of soldiers, while denying them to Rome.

But the desperately hard trip over the snow- and ice-covered Alps cost him many soldiers, and the northern tribes did not come to his aid. Still, by superior tactics and skill, Hannibal's forces succeeded in wiping out one huge Roman army after another. In a dreadful battle at Cannae in 216 B.C., at least 50,000 Romans died, while Hannibal's losses were about 5,000. But year after year, the Romans held on with dogged persistence, raising new armies and keeping a strong hold on their allies, who remained loyal. This demonstrates how well the Romans had built their system of allies throughout the peninsula.

For about fifteen years Hannibal badgered Rome—maintaining himself and his forces in a hostile land, hoping for reinforcements from home that never reached him, never losing a major battle but never able to take Rome.

At last, in 204 B.C., the Roman general Scipio and an army sailed for Africa, to attack Hannibal's home city of Carthage. Hannibal and his troops followed, and at the battle of Zama, in 202 B.C., Hannibal was defeated and the war was at an end. Under the

Herakles—one of the most important heroes in Greek mythology —became the Roman Hercules, shown here after performing the labor of slaying the Erymanthian boar.

peace treaty, concluded in 201 B.C., Rome gained control of the whole western Mediterranean region.

In 149 B.C. the Third Punic War broke out—after Carthage attacked an ally of Rome. Rome sent an army to Africa and, after a three-year seige, Carthage was captured. The few survivors were enslaved, and the city was completely leveled and then plowed under, and the furrows were sown with salt to create a wasteland. The Romans then established a new province, called Africa, in the lands the Carthaginians had once ruled.

Even during the period of the Punic Wars, Rome was also involved in other external wars and, always victorious, was spreading its control eastward, through other lands. Rome fought two wars (214–196 B.C.) against Philip V of Macedon, invaded Asia to fight Antiochus III of Syria (191–189 B.C.), and conquered Greece. By 146 B.C. the whole Mediterranean could be called a Roman "lake."

TROUBLE IN THE STATE

The many years of war left scars all through Italy. Towns were destroyed, thousands of farms neglected and ruined, society disrupted. Some people had grown rich through the war, and they bought out the small, poor farmers who could not afford to restore their farms. This was the beginning of huge estates in Italy. The owners used gangs of slaves (mostly prisoners of war) to work their large farms, instead of free workers. The returning soldiers who had no farms to return to, the displaced former landowners, and others, drifted into the towns—where there was no work either. The Romans may have won their wars, but they were badly hurt by them.

By the second century B.C., Rome was ready to explode under the pressure of social, political, and economic problems. Now a number of leaders emerged, each eager to reorganize the state in a different way. The brothers Tiberius and Gaius Gracchus (called the Gracchi) were among the first reformers. Tiberius was elected to serve as a tribune in 133 B.C. He tried to get small plots of public land distributed for use by the poor. The Senate, made up of many wealthy landowners, was not willing to do this. A riot was arranged in which Tiberius and his followers were killed. This ugly political murder demonstrated the growing corruption of the Senate and its lack of concern for the people.

But Tiberius Gracchus's attempts at reform had popular support, and eleven years later his brother, Gaius, was elected tribune. He proposed even more sweeping land and social reforms. And he, too, was destroyed, along with his supporters.

The last century of the Republic was so filled with disorder and political strife that some historians call it the Roman Revolution. The Senate became weaker and more corrupt; the assemblies too were powerless. Class divisions grew more bitter, and discontent swelled among the common people. Only ambitious and strong-willed military leaders seemed able to gain power—each holding it for a time. Two of the most important were Marius and Sulla. Marius was a successful general who was elected to seven terms as consul. By opening the ranks of the army to landless people, he changed it from a legion of citizens to a professional standing army, with its greatest loyalty to its commanders, not the state. Marius's rival, Sulla, gained fame in the bloody two-year Social War (from the word *socii*, meaning "allies"). In 90 B.C., Rome's Italian allies tried to secede from Rome. Sulla crushed the revolt, but Rome had to grant citizenship to the allies. As Marius and Sulla vied for power, they paid little attention to the welfare of the state. And after Marius and Sulla, other military leaders would soon reach for power—Crassus, Pompey, and Caesar.

JULIUS CAESAR AND HIS TIME

In 60 B.C. three strong, ambitious men—each hoping for power and glory—joined together to achieve their goals in what came to be called the First Triumvirate (from the Latin *trium*, "of three," plus *viri*, "men"). The three, Pompey, Crassus, and Caesar, did not try to seize the government; they planned, by working together, to influence and control its actions.

Pompey (106–48 B.C.) was a popular and successful general who had built his reputation by putting down a revolt in Spain, clearing the eastern Mediterranean of pirates in just ninety days, and finally ending a twenty-five year battle against King Mithridates of Pontus in Asia Minor. Crassus (115–53 B.C.) was said to be the richest person in Rome. He had gained fame as the commander who crushed a revolt of gladiators and slaves led by the courageous gladiator Spartacus, in 71 B.C. Gaius Julius Caesar (100?–44 B.C.) was a rising and restless young leader. He had just returned from a military success in Spain and was eager for power.

For a few years the arrangement worked well. Caesar became consul in 59 B.C. The next year he left his allies in Rome, while he went off to serve as commander in Gaul, a region in Europe that included France, Belgium, and Germany west of the Rhine. In the nine years Caesar spent in Gaul, he proved himself an able and determined military leader. He began his conquests by subduing a

Statues of Julius Caesar were erected throughout the Roman lands. This one, from the Roman colony near modern Turin, was flanked by two sixteen-sided towers in the wall of the city.

Celtic tribe of Switzerland, the Helvetians. Then he learned that Germanic tribes, under Ariovistus and other leaders, were crossing the Rhine into Gaul. He decided to march across the Rhine himself, to frighten the Germans by the sight of Rome's strength. He built a great bridge over the river, the foundations of which still exist.

Caesar also found that the Gauls were being helped and encouraged by tribes in Britain. So he made two trips across the English Channel, in 55 and 54 B.C., to show his might there.

In 52 B.C., when Caesar thought he had conquered all of Gaul, the Gallic tribes united for the first time and rebelled. Their leader was the chieftain Vercingetorix. Caesar cornered his forces in the fortress town of Alesia and, after a long and bitter siege, starved them into surrender. Now all of Gaul was Roman. This conquest was an achievement that would influence the world from that day to ours, for it began the Romanization of western Europe—as the Latin language and Roman law, thought, religion, and culture became dominant in the region.

Caesar's years in Gaul brought him wealth and the backing of a strong, experienced, and loyal army. He had also achieved fame at home. Through the course of his campaigns, he had sent back regular reports about himself and his conquests. These straightforward, vigorous, and remarkably effective reports became famous as the *Commentaries on the Gallic War.* Caesar's accounts of his victories thrilled the people of Rome, and they are still widely read today.

Acclaimed, wealthy, and powerful, Caesar was ready to return to Rome. But not everyone rejoiced at his coming. The Triumvirate had crumbled. Crassus had died in 53 B.C. while leading an army in Syria. Pompey had grown alarmed at Caesar's growing success and began to work to turn the Senate against him.

In 49 B.C., the Senate backed Pompey against Caesar and ordered him to disband his army. They declared him a public enemy. Two tribunes who supported Caesar—Mark Antony and Cassius—feared for their lives in angry and divided Rome, and fled to join Caesar. When Caesar heard of the Senate's order, he decided to act. He was camped with his army on the bank of the Rubicon, a river in northern Italy that divided the province he governed from Italy. Under Roman law, to cross the boundaries of his province with his army was treason against the state. Caesar boldly led his 5,000 soldiers across the river and began to march on Rome, making his bid for power and plunging the state into a civil war.

Pompey and many senators fled before Caesar and went to Greece, planning to mount a campaign there. But Caesar swept through Italy in sixty days, gaining new troops and public support, and moved from Italy to Spain, and then to Greece. At the battle of Pharsalus, in 48 B.C., he routed Pompey's forces. Pompey again fled, this time to Egypt. Caesar followed, but found Pompey had been slain.

Caesar was now master of Italy, but many of its provinces were still in his enemies' hands. In Egypt, Caesar met and fell in love with the young queen, Cleopatra, and was persuaded to help place her firmly on the throne. He then returned to the task of bringing all the Roman provinces under his control. In 47 B.C., he crushed Pharnaces II, king of Pontos, and sent the Senate the short, forceful dispatch: *"Veni, vidi, vici"* ("I came, I saw, I conquered"). In 46 B.C., at Thapsos in northern Africa, and in 45 B.C., at Munda, Caesar defeated the remnants of Pompey's supporters and his sons.

Caesar could now turn to restoring the state. He had himself appointed dictator of Rome for ten years, and was later named dictator for life. Much of his power he used wisely to attack the many social, economic, and political problems that faced Rome. He restored law and order and improved the system of governing the provinces and of collecting taxes. The right of citizenship was offered to many provincials, including the Gauls. Thousands of former soldiers were set up on small land holdings throughout Italy, and new colonies were founded outside Italy. This relieved overcrowding in Rome and, along with public projects, provided work for many citizens. He built temples, a theater, and other buildings, and founded a large public library of the best works in Greek and Latin. With the help of a Greek astronomer, he created a new calendar. Each year was to have 365 days; every fourth year had an extra day. His calendar—called the Julian calendar—has continued to be used with minor changes to the present. Caesar planned to have a census taken and to have the Roman laws classified and written down. He was remarkable for his military and administrative ability, his decisiveness, his strong personality, and his generous and fair treatment of former enemies. He was a master of prose literature and a clear, forceful writer.

Even while Caesar was being hailed as Father of the Country, feelings against the absolute dictator were rising. Some Romans envied Caesar, while others feared him. Many resented him for having assumed total power and blamed him for destroying the Republic. A group of senators formed a conspiracy against him. Among the leaders were "noble" (as Shakespeare described him) Brutus, an idealistic supporter of the Republic; and "lean and hungry" Cassius. As Caesar entered a meeting of the Senate in Rome on the Ides of March, March 15, 44 B.C., the conspirators stabbed him to death.

The chaotic era of Pompey, Crassus, and Caesar was not marked only by brutal struggles for power. It was also a time of intellectual development, and it saw the appearance of gifted poets, philosophers, and historians. Perhaps the greatest of these was Cicero—a giant figure who embodied the culture of the last period of the Republic. If Caesar is set aside, it is Cicero who appears the most characteristic and brilliant person of the age; he stood for what was best in Latin thinking and writing.

Marcus Tullius Cicero (106–43 B.C.) was one of the greatest prose writers and orators of the ancient world, and a steadfast champion of the Roman Republic and its constitution. He received some of his education at Athens, then returned to Rome, where he entered public life, dedicating himself, at first, to law.

He rose quickly, held many important offices, and was elected consul in 63 B.C. He then exposed a conspiracy to capture the government by force that was led by the bitter, ambitious Catiline. In four brilliant, emotional speeches, he warned the Romans of Catiline's plot and saved the state.

Oratory—the art of speaking effectively and persuasively—was prized in Rome. Schools to teach orators, based on Greek models, appeared in Rome from 95 B.C. Oratory was an essential part of the training for young, ambitious Romans, as a means of self-expression and as a tool for political competition. Cicero may well have won his consulship by his masterful style; Caesar was said to be second to no one but Cicero.

Today we have fifty-eight of Cicero's speeches, and about 900 of his witty, humorous, and wise letters to friends. They give us a vivid picture of Rome in his day. The personalities and crises are shown in detail, and so are Cicero's reactions to them. He was sometimes influenced to change sides on a question, but on important issues, he held firmly to his beliefs.

Cicero also wrote a number of philosophical works, the most famous of which is the *Republic*. In it, he suggests what he thinks is necessary for orderly government. He believed the officers of the state should work peacefully together with the help of the leading citizens.

After Caesar was killed, Cicero fought with all his strength against Mark Antony, Caesar's successor, in hopes of saving the Republic—the form of government he supported. In 43 B.C. he was killed by soldiers of Mark Antony.

Among the other great Romans of this time was Catullus (87–54 B.C.), who wrote fine lyric poetry. Another poet, Lucretius (99–55 B.C.), in the long work *On the Nature of Things*, tried to explain evolution through the movement of atoms. Varro (116–27 B.C.) was a writer and a prominent Roman scholar. He wrote hundreds of books, including encyclopedic studies of Roman life, religion, agriculture, biography, and nearly every other subject, from music to geography.

AUGUSTUS AND THE ROMAN EMPIRE

Caesar's murder was followed by another bitter struggle for power. Out of this clash, two men emerged as rival leaders—Mark Antony (82–30 B.C.), Caesar's friend and officer; and Octavian (63 B.C.–A.D. 14), who was Caesar's grand-nephew and adopted heir. They then faced each other in a final contest. Antony had gone to Egypt to live with his new wife, Queen Cleopatra. Octavian remained in Rome. Their struggle erupted into war between Rome and Egypt. In 31 B.C., their fleets met in the Bay of Actium, in northwestern Greece. Here, Octavian won a decisive victory. Antony and Cleopatra fled to Egypt, where they committed suicide.

One man now stood supreme in the Roman world. In 27 B.C. the Roman Senate and people proclaimed him their ruler. The Senate gave him the title Augustus, which means "the revered one," and Octavian is called by this name from this point on.

So the Roman Republic came to an end and its place was taken by the Roman Empire. Augustus, the emperor, claimed that he had "restored" the Republic, but this was a pretense. He used the title *princeps* ("the first"), meaning the first citizen of the state, since this title was more suited to the leader of a republic than *rex* ("king") or dictator. But the use of *princeps* and his other efforts to keep the old republican forms—such as having the people elect the consuls and having the Senate continue—could not hide the

fact that Augustus held all real power himself and was, in truth, emperor.

Augustus ruled for a long time, from 27 B.C. to A.D. 14. While his rule did not allow the people of Rome true liberty, it did bring them peace and prosperity. His forty-one year reign opened the period called the *Pax Romana* ("Roman Peace"), which lasted over 200 years. There were some disturbances and border conflicts during this time, but no prolonged war. And even after the peace was finally destroyed, the Empire itself was strong enough to continue on for several centuries.

Augustus was given the credit for the flourishing economy, and the contentment that spread through the vast Roman world. He restored law and security and introduced many reforms. He improved the system of taxation and, for the first time, set up a fair and efficient system of government for the provinces. To run the everyday business of governing, he created a civil service—made up of able administrators, chosen by merit. He beautified the cities and began Rome's first public police and fire-fighting forces. The standard of living improved, business thrived, and people could travel easily throughout the Empire.

Egypt was now part of the Roman Empire. Rome soon ruled the whole world from Britain to the Euphrates River in Mesopotamia (in modern Iraq). The entire Mediterranean was Roman. In Europe, the frontiers ran along the Rhine and Danube Rivers; in Africa, along the Sahara Desert; in Asia, along the Euphrates River. Across the Euphrates was the Parthian Empire, the only advanced state that did not belong to Rome. China was too far away to be part of Rome's thinking, although there was trade between the two states.

**Statues of the Emperor
Augustus portray him as
the noble bringer of peace.**

Through his reforms, Augustus put the vast Empire into order, with one uniform system of government throughout Rome and the provinces. Now a uniform system of law was needed, to function throughout the Empire. Roman law had its beginnings in the early days of the Republic, about 450 B.C., when the plebeians had demanded that the patricians draw up a code of law—so that all could know the laws of the state and so they could be applied equally to all. The result—a simple, logical listing of the laws and rules about property, customs, and rights—was called the Twelve Tables, for it was written on twelve wooden tablets. This served as a base for Roman law through the centuries. Under Augustus, laws were adapted to Rome's new position and needs and were introduced throughout the Empire. Much later, in the sixth century A.D., the Emperor Justinian ordered the whole body of Roman law to be organized and classified. This work is called the Justinian Code.

Roman law was concerned above all with the rights of individuals. It recognized the rights of people to their property. It held that people could will their goods to whomever they wished; it insisted that an agreement in writing is binding. It was a humane law and said that a person is innocent until proved guilty, and it was respected and obeyed by all the people.

ART IN THE AUGUSTAN AGE

In working to restore the state, Augustus tried to revive the people's interest in religion. He hoped that by a return to the old virtues and piety, the state would be strengthened. He built and repaired many temples to the gods, reinstated religious festivals, and urged the Romans to worship the gods of the state, such as Jupiter. But the days of the old state religion could not be recovered. People were dissatisfied with the cold, formal gods; and too often, religion and politics had been joined together. In addition, other religions were competing for the attention and devotion of the people. Among these were Judaism and the new religion Christianity.

Augustus also tried to strengthen family ties, to make marriage bonds stronger, and to lessen the opportunity for divorce. He passed laws governing the morals of the people. Artists, poets and historians, and others were encouraged to help build public morality, and many did, through their works, promote these ideas.

The greatest Roman poet was Virgil (70–19 B.C.). He was deeply moved by Rome's traditions and splendid history. His long epic poem the *Aeneid* (from the poem's hero, Aeneas) celebrated the founding of Rome and foretold the glorious reign of its future ruler Augustus. Virgil's story is lively and dramatic. It shows that Rome's great successes—which won a world state—were the

About 9 B.C., the Senate erected the Altar of Peace,
a shrine to honor the peace of the Augustan Age.
Its beautifully carved reliefs—one of the
greatest art works of the time—portray members
of Augustus's family and officials of the state.

result of a stern regard for duty. Virgil, more perfectly than any other writer, expressed the noble and patriotic ideals of Augustan Rome. He is widely read today.

Another famous writer of the time was the lyric poet and satirist Horace (65–8 B.C.). Horace told his readers to forget the civil wars that ended the Roman Republic. Think of the present and enjoy your life, he said, and leave the future to the gods. He recommended good friends, a comfortable house, and fine food as the best things of life. For hundreds of years people have enjoyed Horace's *Odes*, four books of accomplished poetry, filled with humor, passion, and artistry.

Much of our knowledge of Greek and Roman mythology comes from another Augustan poet, Ovid (43 B.C.–A.D. 17). His *Metamorphoses* is a great historical epic and provides a wealth of information about the gods.

Among the writers of prose in the Augustan Age, one of the most famous is Livy (59 B.C.–A.D. 17). Livy wrote a moving and dramatic history of Rome from its beginnings. Some of it is lost, but the parts that remain are the most valuable—but not fully reliable—source we have for early Roman history. Livy, and the later Tacitus (c. A.D. 55–116), the great historian of the Empire, rank as Rome's most important historians. Livy portrayed the brilliance of Rome's early days and glorified its people and their deeds, hoping to provide a moral influence for his audience.

In the days of Augustus, as in other days, writers and artists needed financial support and encouragement. The person who provided the most help was a wealthy and generous lover of the arts, Maecenas (d. 8 B.C.). He was a friend and trusted advisor to Augustus. Even today a patron of the arts may be called a Maecenas.

Much of the genius of the Romans found expression in fine buildings and beautiful cities. A great deal of the building activity during the Augustan Age went on in the Roman Forum and its neighborhood. The Forum had begun as a simple marketplace,

The stately temple called the Pantheon was
first built by Agrippa and rebuilt by Hadrian
in the second century A.D. The inscription
across the front tells us: Agrippa made this,
in his third term as consul.

but by the time of Augustus it was a busy center of the city. Here were the Public Records Office, basilicas (public buildings), and the Temple of Concord (Unity). A Sacred Way—used for religious processions and processions of triumphal generals—led through arches down the Forum to the speaker's platform. Even before Augustus the Roman Forum had become so crowded with its buildings and statues that Julius Caesar built his own Forum nearby. Augustus added a third Forum. Another center of building activity was in the Campus Martius, or Field of Mars, a level stretch of land beside the Tiber.

Under Augustus, much of the building activity was directed by Agrippa (63–12 B.C.), the emperor's friend and aide, and an able engineer. He built aqueducts to ensure an adequate water supply for Rome, public baths, and the original temple called the Pantheon. This building burned down twice and was then rebuilt by the Emperor Hadrian in the second century. Its dome shows the daring of the Roman engineers, for it was made of solid concrete, with a diameter of 142 feet (43.3 m) and 142 feet high. The only natural light for the building came through a 30-foot (9.1-m) round opening in the center of the dome. The outside of the dome was once covered with tiles of gilded bronze, so it could be seen, gleaming, from any part of Rome.

Hadrian's other great buildings also remain as landmarks today—his tomb, now known as the Castel Sant' Angelo, and his lavish villa in Tivoli, outside the city of Rome.

The Roman architects and engineers took many of their artistic ideas from the Greeks and the Etruscans, and then adapted them to their own practical use. Nowhere are we more impressed by their skill—and by the might and wealth of the Roman Empire—than on the Palatine Hill. Here Augustus and later emperors constructed enormous, stately palaces.

Basilicas were built throughout Rome. They were state buildings and were used as courts of justice and as public or social meeting places, and for commerce. The interior was usually divided into a broad central hall, and narrow aisles to the side. There was sometimes a semicircular wall, or apse, at one end and, sometimes, a raised platform. In time, the early Christians turned many basilicas into churches and also used the basilica design when they built new churches.

One of the most beautiful monuments of the Augustan Age is the Altar of Peace. It is richly decorated with objects suggesting prosperity, such as flowers and fruit. It shows Augustus and members of his family marching with priests and magistrates to the sacrifices in honor of peace.

Practical Romans preferred realism in their art. We see this in their magnificent portrait sculpture, and on their coins and gems. Many successful Roman generals brought home shiploads of statues from Greece, and these, too, influenced Roman taste. The Romans decorated arches and columns with carved scenes of historical events.

Although Rome itself was the center of culture in the Augustan Age, the provinces, too, showed the greatness of the mighty Empire. From one end of the Empire to the other stretched large and beautiful cities. In ancient times, Asia Minor boasted 500 cities. All these cities were modeled after Rome. Each had its own forums, temples, triumphal arches, basilicas, and aqueducts. Fine paved roads united the cities.

Some of the largest cities were in the East, such as Alexandria in Egypt and Antioch in Syria. Other great cities were built on the very edges of ancient civilization. Bath, set among the forests of Britain, was a famous Roman watering place, or vacation resort. Timgad, beside the Sahara Desert, Palmyra, an oasis in the Syrian Desert, Petra, in northern Arabia, all have remains of Roman cities.

Impressive as these great cities were, even more impressive is the fact that to protect this huge world the Romans used an army of only 400,000 men. And most of them were stationed along the frontiers, on guard against the barbarian tribes of central Europe, and, in the East, against Parthia.

DAILY LIFE IN ROME

The head of the Roman family was the father. In the early days of Rome he had absolute authority, even the power of life and death, over his wife and children. Later this power was broken, but the family remained a close group for a long time. All the members of the family worshipped the gods and studied the stories of Rome's great past together.

Women were respected and had responsibility for overseeing their households and raising children. They attended public ceremonies and were not secluded. By the end of the Republic they had more rights; for example, they could own property in their own names.

Young Roman children first attended an elementary school where they learned reading, writing, and arithmetic. Boys then entered a higher school and studied both Greek and Latin literature and history, and memorized some of Rome's more important laws. Girls continued learning at home.

If his parents could afford it, a Roman boy was then taught by a tutor. This was often a Greek slave who had been captured in a war. He might then finish his education in Athens, which was a sort of university center. Educated Romans continued to read throughout their lives.

Upon his return home to Rome, the young man practiced oratory. A good speaker had the best chance of being elected to pub-

lic office, and many ambitious youths hoped to someday become a consul.

When he reached the age of twenty-five or thirty, a Roman was ready for marriage. His marriage was arranged with the father of the prospective bride, since she was usually too young to be consulted in the matter. Then too, she was under her father's control.

The marriage ceremonies began with a feast and a sacrifice in the house of the bride's father. They ended in the evening with a grand procession to the groom's home. Here the bride was carefully lifted over the threshold, for it was considered bad luck if she stumbled over the sill of her new home.

Life in the family was disciplined and happy. Simplicity was the rule, and it is seen by the clothing worn by Romans generation after generation. Both men and women wore a tunic, a plain garment, usually of wool, that came down to the knees. If a man was going to a public meeting, he probably threw over this a toga, a loosely fitting garment that would have a purple stripe on it if its wearer was a noble. Cloaks were worn in cold weather.

We have learned a good deal about Roman houses from the excavations at Herculaneum and Pompeii. These two towns were located near the Bay of Naples on the slopes of Mt. Vesuvius, which is still an active volcano. In the year A.D. 79 Vesuvius erupted and buried the nearby towns under a mass of ashes and lava. Apparently the ashes came down on Pompeii in two stages. During the first, many people escaped, but some returned, when the ashes stopped falling, to get their jewels. Then the second stage began, and these people were buried.

Villas were often decorated with murals, such as this one showing the woman of the house playing a cithara, watched (perhaps) by her daughter.

[39]

Many of the houses in Pompeii, as in other
Roman towns, had small rooms facing the street
which were used as shops, such as this bakery
with flour mills of volcanic stone.

We know this because archeologists, in excavating the ancient city, found the outlines of people sometimes halfway out of windows, with money or jewels in their hands. The archeologists poured plaster of paris into the outlines of these bodies, and visitors to Pompeii today can see plaster casts of people who once lived there.

Pompeii is an almost unbelievable sight, a vast dead city, with private houses, temples, and public buildings. There are paved streets with ruts, stepping-stones, small shops, and restaurants. Some ancient water pipes still work, so that the fountains at the crossings of streets and inside the courtyards of houses still play. Moreover, archeologists have identified from their roots the bushes and trees that once grew in Pompeii. They have planted the same bushes and trees again, just as they grew in ancient days.

The typical Roman house, in Pompeii and Rome and elsewhere, did not look very exciting from the street. The walls were plain and windowless. The first room you came to was the *atrium*, a main hall and living room, which received light from an opening in the roof above. When it rained, the water that poured through the opening fell into a basin or *impluvium*, which had a fountain and statues and sometimes held goldfish. The floors of a Roman living room were decorated with small pieces of colored stone and glass called mosaics. The walls were painted with brightly colored scenes or designs. Surrounding the atrium were rooms where the family records and portraits of ancestors were kept. Next were bedrooms and sometimes a dining room. Small rooms facing onto the public street were used as shops.

Food was prepared in the kitchen by slaves—for every household, except the poorest, had slaves. The stoves burned wood, and the kettles, frying pans, and other utensils were much like ours. Bread, cheese, and olives were the chief foods, although a moderately prosperous family would have fish, meat, poultry, and green vegetables as well. Honey was used for sweetening, and wine was served with the main meal, *cena*, or "dinner," in the late afternoon.

[41]

Because of the warm climate, the family's life centered in the courtyard around which the house was built. This courtyard was open to the sky. It had columns around it which provided a shaded walk. In the center was often a fountain, circled by flower beds, bushes, and even trees.

This type of house belonged to a prosperous middle-class family. Rich, fashionable people owned large estates and fine houses in the country. The poor were crowded into city tenements, called *insulae* ("islands"), 60 feet (18.3 m) high. Slaves lived in cramped quarters in the rear of their owner's house or in the cellar.

Most Romans made their living through agriculture. Cereals, grapes, and olives were the most important crops. Nearly all food was grown locally, because transportation was slow. But manufactured articles, such as jewelry, pottery, glass, and bricks, were carried easily over the fine Roman roads, to be sold in cities and provinces.

There was a fine network of roads stretching throughout the Roman world, not only for the use of travelers and the movement of armies, but also for the postal service and commerce. Portions of these roads are still used. The most famous Roman road was the Appian Way, which ran south from the city of Rome. It was constructed with large blocks of stone, and even today cars speed along parts of it.

In the Mediterranean the Romans had a regular boat service. The sea journey from Rome to Egypt took three weeks and was the most important of all the services. This was because Rome imported much of its wheat from Egypt, and the poorer people in Rome might riot if the grain supply fell low.

The Appian Way, the chief highway of ancient Rome, was lined with family tombstones along its sides.

The population of the Roman Empire at its height numbered about 100 million, with a million of these people living in the city of Rome itself. Here in the capital was the whole apparatus of government. The many officials lived here. The chief temples and other public buildings were located in Rome.

Rome was also the entertainment center of the Empire. The Circus Maximus, for example, was used for horse races. It was the largest of ancient stadiums and seated over 150,000 persons. The largest of the many Roman theaters was the Colosseum, with a seating capacity of about 50,000. Rome also had more than 800 public baths scattered around the city. A Roman bath had hot, warm, and cold pools, but it was much more than a bathing establishment. It was a social meeting place, with libraries and lecture halls, racecourses, gardens, and rooms for wrestling and boxing.

The business of government and of trade, the lively entertainments, and the free food the government provided for the poor, attracted people from all over the world to Rome. Rome had become the capital of the world.

THE EMPIRE AFTER AUGUSTUS

The first rulers who followed Augustus came from within his own family and that of his third wife, Livia. The solid foundation he had established for the state carried it through the reigns of his successors—from the efficient but brutal Tiberius (r. A.D. 14–37), the cruel, incompetent Caligula (r. A.D. 37–41), and the steady Claudius (r. A.D. 41–54) to the rule of Nero (r. A.D. 54–68).

Nero began his rule well but soon turned it into a cruel tyranny, with himself as dictator. He murdered his half-brother, his mother, and his wife. He filled Rome with spies who informed on the activities of the people. When Rome burned in A.D. 64, the story (now held untrue) spread that Nero had started it and had watched, playing on his lyre and singing of the burning of Troy. Nero blamed the Christians for the fire. His reign of terror continued until Rome's armies rebelled and Nero committed suicide.

During this time there had been no set rule by which an emperor was chosen. After Nero's death, a civil war erupted between supporters of rival candidates. In the second century, the Romans developed a method of choosing their emperors. Each reigning emperor selected the ablest person he could find and adopted that person as his successor. The result was that during the second century, Rome had fine, respected rulers—called the five "good emperors."

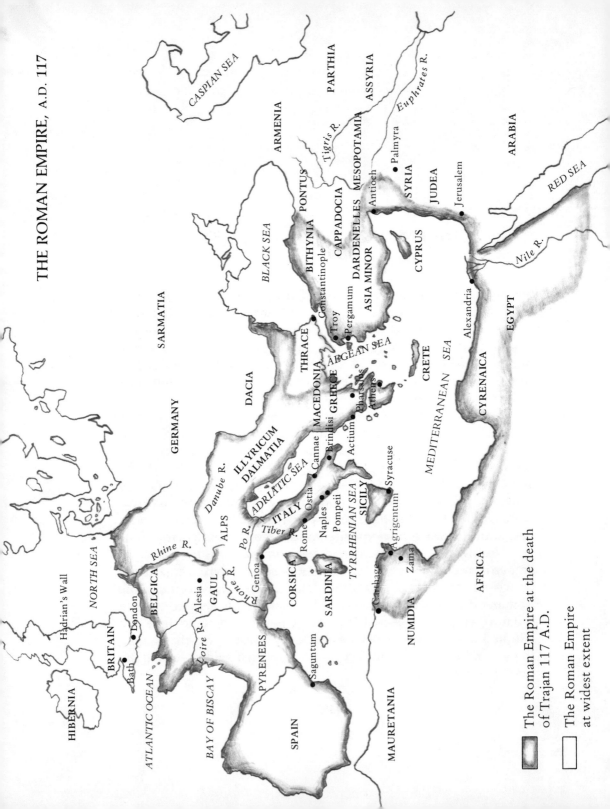

THE ROMAN EMPIRE, A.D. 117

The Roman Empire at the death of Trajan 117 A.D.

The Roman Empire at widest extent

Trajan (r. A.D. 98–117) enlarged the Empire in one important area. The barbarian tribes of Central Europe were pressing against the lower Danube, where that great river makes a bend southward. Trajan crossed the river, conquered the district, and made it a province. In those days it was called Dacia, but Roman civilization took such deep root there that ever since it has been called Romania. As a memorial to his victory Trajan erected a tall column in the Forum he built at Rome. Today it is a landmark of Rome.

Hadrian (r. A.D. 117–138), the next emperor, also was concerned with preserving the defenses of the Empire. He discovered that in Britain the Picts of Caledonia—or Scotland, as we call it—were raiding the Roman province. So he built a great wall to keep them out. Hadrian traveled continually throughout the Empire. This showed his subjects that it was the whole Roman world, not just the city of Rome, that was important. Wherever he went, Hadrian constructed buildings. Unfortunately, all this cost a good deal, and so did the task of running the government. People found it difficult to pay the necessary taxes.

The reign of Hadrian is often described as the high point of the Roman Empire. A person who lived during Hadrian's time called the whole world a paradise, where people might travel safely by land and sea from one end of the Empire to the other—from Britain to Arabia; where, in place of war, cities competed with each other only in their splendor and pleasures. One culture, one system of law, covered the Empire.

During the rule of Marcus Aurelius (r. A.D. 161–180), the Roman Peace ended. He was an educated, sensitive man and a devoted follower of the Stoic philosophy. This philosophy preached of the importance of right conduct, integrity, and self-reliance, and of the community of all humankind. Marcus Aurelius wrote at great length of his search for self-knowledge, using Greek—the language of his teachers and of the first Stoics. His notes, called the *Meditations*, were written at night, by campfires,

The Colosseum, planned by Augustus and built later
by the Emperor Vespasian, provided an amphitheater
large enough to allow many thousands of spectators
to see the gladiator contests and other displays.

for the barbarian tribes were attacking the Empire and were pressing hard from the east and the west. Marcus spent most of his reign marching from one frontier to another, to drive back the invaders. At the same time, a terrible plague (perhaps smallpox) broke out and raged for years. Famine also stalked the Empire.

The peaceful, prosperous days of Augustus were gone. When Marcus died in A.D. 180, the Empire was under many great strains. And, unfortunately, he ignored the principle of choosing the ablest person as heir, and named his son Commodus (r. A.D. 180–192) as his successor. With the rule of this dull, savage emperor, began the Empire's decline. He was the first of many tyrants, as troubles swelled for a hundred years. During a seventy-four-year period, after Commodus, there were twenty-seven emperors, some of whom ruled for only a day or two before they were murdered. When the hope of self-government had died, along with the Republic, an important balance was lost from the Roman state. There was no longer an Assembly or a Senate with the power to stand up to or stop the emperor, who had become an absolute monarch. A weak, evil, or stupid ruler could severely damage the state.

During these dark years, the Empire began to crumble. In Africa, in the East, along the Rhine, in Gaul, and in Spain, the enemies of Rome continued to attack. Trade declined, money fell in value, the armies rebelled. The constant wars drained the economy and the spirit of the people.

As the Roman Empire weakened, various religions gained strength. Since a happy life on earth was no longer possible for many people, they began to hope for a better life in the world to come, or to search for gods that might be more powerful than their own. Beginning in the first century A.D., many religions came out of the East and attracted the Romans. Mithraism, a mystery religion that promised immortality, was one of the most important. It had appeared in Rome even in the days of the Republic, and now became widely popular. Christianity gained followers.

The Romans were generally tolerant of religions other than the state religion, as long as the worshipper agreed to make sacrifices to the Roman emperor. But the Christians, who refused to do this, were resented and persecuted.

CONSTANTINE AND CHRISTIANITY

The barbarian invasions of the Roman Empire during the third century finally came to an end. The emperor Diocletian (r. A.D. 284–305) succeeded in gathering the reins of government firmly in his hands and establishing peace and order. His reforms strengthened the state and enabled the Empire to hold together for 200 years more. But the Roman world was never the same. The emperors no longer even pretended to rule with the advice of the Senate, or anyone else. The people of the Empire now lived under a despotic government.

After Diocletian there was again a struggle for power. One who claimed the right to rule was Constantine (r. A.D. 306–337). On his march to Rome, to meet and battle a rival, it was reported that he had a vision of a Christian cross with the words, "By this sign conquer." He was victorious, and in gratitude made Christianity the state religion.

Constantine the Great is called Rome's first Christian emperor. He moved the capital from Rome to the old Greek city of Byzantium, on the Bosporus, in what is now Turkey. It was rebuilt as a Christian city and renamed Constantinople. Today it is called Istanbul.

The cost of the new capital and its decoration, and the expenses of his large army and many officials, were tremendous.

To meet them, Constantine taxed the people heavily. Many farmers, unable to pay their tax, fled to the cities where they would not be so easily noticed by the tax collectors.

As more and more farmers deserted their land, the Empire was threatened with famine. For that reason Constantine decreed that farmers must remain on their land. This was the beginning of the serfdom of the next centuries, whereby people were bound to the soil and subject to the will of the person who owned it.

Constantine had wanted a new capital because he was eager to leave Rome, with its reminders of a more democratic past. He thought, too, that as a dictator he should have his own imperial capital. He placed it in the East because that was closest to the lower Danube and Euphrates rivers, where the chief danger of barbarian invasion seemed to lie.

In the years ahead the barbarians kept pressing on the frontiers and occasionally got across and raided the Empire. Alaric and the Goths, the Vandals, and Attila the Hun from northern Europe were some of the worst invaders. In A.D. 395 the Roman Empire split into Western and Eastern halves. The Western Roman Empire grew steadily weaker and then, in A.D. 476, went down completely before the barbarians. German chieftains sat on the throne of Augustus. Europe was broken up into different kingdoms and entered a new phase of history, that of the Middle Ages. The bishop of Rome, known as the pope, did what he could to protect the people of the West from harsh barbarian rule.

The Eastern Roman Empire, however, with its capital at Constantinople, survived the onslaught of the barbarians. In fact, it stood until 1453, when the Ottoman Turks finally overwhelmed this last stronghold of the ancient world.

**The Arch of Constantine
was built to honor the
Emperor's victory over
a rival in A.D. 312.**

ROME'S LEGACY

Although the Roman Empire fell, it continues to live. Its culture and way of life have survived and are part of our world today.

When Rome built its empire and spread its ideas, language, system of laws, beliefs, literature, and architectural styles through all the remote parts of its realm—"Romanizing" the world—it insured its survival. And when the barbarian tribespeople who became the new rulers of the Western Roman Empire accepted Christianity, they adopted much of Roman civilization too.

We call the civilization Roman, but in fact it was a mixed culture. The Romans were very successful borrowers, adapters, and preservers. The culture they passed on contained a great deal that came from the ancient Greeks, some from the Etruscans, the Jews, the Persians, and others—all filtered through the Roman mind.

The Roman legacy to us is enormous, and has become so essential a part of our world that it is sometimes hard to recognize. The Christian religion—which was later to preserve much of Roman culture—is one of Rome's most important legacies. The Roman concept of law and justice and the rights of individuals is the base upon which much of our system of justice was built. The Roman traditions of republicanism and their ability to structure and order a state are valued today. The Latin language survives in the Church and among scholars today. In addition, it developed into Italian, Spanish, French, Portuguese, and Romanian and was the source of many English words. Architecture, literature, art, and philosophy are all richer for the contributions of the ancient Romans.

WORDS FROM THE ROMANS

Agriculture. The growing of crops. From the Latin *agricultura*: *ager* ("field") plus *cultura* ("cultivation"); cultivation of the field.

Ancestor. A person from whom one is descended. From the Latin *antecessor*: *ante* ("before") plus *cedere* ("to go"); one that goes before.

Animal. A living creature. From the Latin *animalis* ("living"), *anima* ("breath"); anything that breathes.

Bisect. To divide into two parts. From the Latin *bi* ("two") plus *secare, sectus* ("to cut").

Cereal. A grain, such as oats or wheat, or a food made from a grain. From the Latin *cerealis* ("of Ceres"). Ceres was the Roman goddess who was the protector of the crops.

Closet. A cupboard or closed area for storing things. From the Latin *clausum* ("a closed place").

Companion. A person who accompanies another. From the Latin *cum* ("with") plus *panis* ("bread"); a person who shares bread or eats with another.

[57]

Conspiracy. A plot or secret plan to perform an illegal or evil act. From the Latin *conspiratio: con* ("together") plus *spiro* ("breathe"); to breathe together, to agree, to plot.

Exit. To go out, or the way out. From the Latin *exitus: ex* ("out") plus *ire* ("to go").

Genius. A person of more than ordinary intelligence or ability. From the Latin *genius* ("a guardian spirit").

Gravity. The pull or force of the earth; also seriousness, importance. From the Latin *gravitas, gravis* ("heavy").

Inch. The twelfth part of a foot. From the Latin *uncia* ("a twelfth part").

Investigate. To look into, or examine. From the Latin *investigare: in* ("in") plus *vestigium* ("footprint"), *vestigare* ("to track from footprints"); to trace out or search into.

Janitor. A person in charge of a building. From the Latin *janua* ("door"); from Janus, the Roman god of gates and doorways.

Manufacture. To make or process into a product. From the Latin *manufactura* ("a making by hand"): *manus* ("hand") plus *facio* ("make"); to make by hand.

Mile. A measure of length. From the Latin *milia, mille* ("a thousand paces").

Object. To protest or oppose. From the Latin *objectum* ("something thrown in the way of"); *ob* ("in the way," "against") plus *jacere* ("to throw"); to throw something in the way of.

Pen. Writing instrument. From the Latin *penna* ("feather"); early writing tools were feathers with the quills sharpened.

Percolator. A coffee pot in which hot water filters through the coffee grounds. From the Latin *percolare* ("to filter through"): *per* ("through") plus *colo* ("filter").

Plant. To place in the ground to grow. From the Latin *planta* ("the sole of the foot"); when seeds were planted, the soil was pressed down with the foot.

Revolution. The overthrow of a government or a system. From the Latin *revolvere* ("to roll back"); *re* ("over") plus *volvo* ("turn"); a rolling back.

Serpent. A snake. From the Latin *serpere, serpentus* ("to creep").

Vacuum. A space entirely devoid of matter. From the Latin *vacuus* ("empty").

Verdict. A decision or judgment. From the Latin *veredictum* ("to speak the truth"): *vere* ("truly") plus *dictum* ("saying").

FOR FURTHER READING

Asimov, Isaac. *The Roman Republic*. Boston: Houghton Mifflin Co., 1966.

Brooks, Polly Schoyer, and Walworth, Nancy Zinsser. *When the World Was Rome, 753 B.C.–A.D. 476*. New York: Lippincott Junior Books, 1972.

Bulfinch, Thomas. *A Book of Myths*. New York: Macmillan Publishing Co., 1942.

Coolidge, Olivia. *Lives of Famous Romans*. Boston: Houghton Mifflin Co., 1965.

Guerber, H.A. *The Myths of Greece and Rome*. Revised by Dorothy Stuart. London: House of Maxwell, 1963.

Hadas, Moses. *Imperial Rome*. New York: Time-Life Books, 1965.

Liversidge, Joan. *Everyday Life in the Roman Empire*. New York: G.P. Putnam's Sons, 1976.

Ruskin, Ariane, and Batterberry, Michael. *Greek and Roman Art*. New York: McGraw-Hill Book Co., 1969.

Virgil. *The Aeneid*. Retold by N. B. Taylor. New York: Henry Z. Walck, Inc., 1961.

INDEX